CHINESE SENTENCE BUILDERS

A lexicogrammar approach

ANSWER BOOK

Absolute Beginners

THE LANGUAGE GYM

About the authors

Chris Webster taught for 15 years, in schools in China and the UK, both in state and independent settings. He lives in Reading, England and has a Master's Degree in teaching with distinction. He is fluent in three languages and knows a smittence of several others. Chris is, besides a teacher, a coder, guitar player, skateboarder, a passionate traveller and a fitness enthusiast. Formerly, Chris was the Programme Director of the Swire Chinese Language Centre Oxford having expanded the teaching of Mandarin to over 25 schools in the region, while supporting and mentoring many other teachers and leaders across the country either on-site or remotely. He was most recently at George Watson's College on secondment. Chris now offers his service as freelance while developing his career in the tech industry.

Maggie Sproule has taught for 18 years, in schools in Singapore and the UK, both in state and independent settings. She lives in Edinburgh, Scotland. She is bilingual and gets by in a few more. She is currently learning Korean – justification or excuse for her binge watching K-dramas! Maggie is also an avid creator of teaching and learning resources, a keen hillwalker and a *makan* enthusiast. In the last couple of years she has been testing and implementing E.P.I. in one of the top Independent schools in Scotland, George Watson's College, where she is currently Principal Teacher of Chinese and the Head of Swire Chinese Language Centre, Edinburgh. As Head of Swire Chinese Language Centre, she has turned what began as a determination to give pupils access to her own first language in the most effective way possible into one of the most successful social and cultural integration projects in Edinburgh.

Gianfranco Conti taught for 25 years at schools in Italy, the UK and in Kuala Lumpur, Malaysia. He has also been a university lecturer, holds a Master's degree in Applied Linguistics and a PhD in metacognitive strategies as applied to second language writing. He is now an author, a popular independent educational consultant and a professional development provider. He has written around 2,000 resources for the TES website, which have awarded him the Best Resources Contributor in 2015. He has co-authored the best-selling and influential book for world languages teachers, "The Language Teacher Toolkit", "Breaking the sound barrier: Teaching learners how to listen", in which he puts forth his Listening As Modelling methodology and "Memory: what every language teacher should know". Last but not least, Gianfranco has created the instructional approach known as E.P.I. (Extensive Processing Instruction).

Dylan Viñales has taught for 15 years, in schools in Bath, Beijing and Kuala Lumpur in state, independent and international settings. He lives in Kuala Lumpur. He is fluent in five languages, and gets by in several more. Dylan is, besides a teacher, a professional development provider, specialising in E.P.I., metacognition, teaching languages through music (especially ukulele) and cognitive science. In the last five years, together with Dr Conti, he has driven the implementation of E.P.I. in one of the top international schools in the world: Garden International School. Dylan authors an influential blog on modern language pedagogy in which he supports the teaching of languages through E.P.I.

DEDICATION

For my parents – Tessa & Kenny
-Chris

For my family – John, Sean & Laura-Beth
-Maggie

For Catrina
-Gianfranco

For Ariella & Leonard
-Dylan

Acknowledgements

Creating a book is a time-consuming yet rewarding endeavour.

Maggie would like to thank her family for all their encouragement and patience while she 'disappears into her computer for hours'. Huge gratitude to colleagues at Swire Chinese Language Centre, Edinburgh for feedback on specific tasks. Secondly, she is grateful to be teaching alongside colleagues at George Watson's College, Edinburgh, who value the importance of the E.P.I approach. A big xiè xie to her pupils for being her crewmates in spotting the 'imposters' in the tasks! I would like to express my sincere gratitude to Gian and Dylan for this fantastic opportunity, to help level the playing field in Chinese language teaching and increase accessibility of Chinese learning.

Chris would like to thank his parents, Tess and Kenny, who have always been there for him through thick and through thin. He would also like to thank Maggie for the same, most sincerely, as having suffered from chronic neck pain for over a year after the writing of our first book, Chris has had to rely heavily on Maggie in helping us get across the line! Chris is indebted to both Dylan and Gian for the faith they have put in us and for helping to bring greater focus to Mandarin, to develop it as a subject and engage teachers to consider other approaches which will benefit students around the world. They are true pioneers!

We would like to thank Andrew and Jessie, for their tireless work, proofreading, recording and editing on this book. They are talented, accomplished professionals who work at the highest possible level and add value at every stage of the process. Your energy, enthusiasm and passion come across clearly in every recording and is the reason why the listening sections are such a successful and engaging resource, according to the many learners who have been alpha and beta testing the book. In addition, both Chris and Maggie would like to express a huge thanks to Andrew for his superb management of the sound editing process. It has been a pleasure to work with these lovely, good-humoured colleagues who go above and beyond, and make the hours of collaborating a real pleasure. Last but not least, our gratitude to Dylan for his moral support and for sharing his expertise of sound recording and digital mastering. Terima kasih! 感恩。

Thanks to Flaticon.com and Mockofun.com for providing access to a limitless library of engaging icons, clipart and images which we have used to make this book more user-friendly than any other Sentence Builders predecessor, with a view to be as engaging as possible for primary level learners.

Finally, our gratitude to the community of teachers of Chinese for their ongoing support of E.P.I. and the Sentence Builders book series. In particular a shoutout to our team of incredible educators who helped in checking all the units: it is thanks to your time, patience, professionalism and detailed feedback that we have been able to produce such a refined and highly accurate product.

感恩,
Maggie, Chris, Gianfranco & Dylan

Introduction

Hello and welcome to the first Sentence Builders workbook designed for absolute beginner, designed to be an accompaniment to a Chinese Extensive Processing Instruction course. The book has come about out of necessity, because such a resource did not previously exist.

How to use this book if you have bought into our E.P.I. approach

This book was originally designed as a resource to use in conjunction with our E.P.I. approach and teaching strategies. Our course favours flooding comprehensible input, organising content by communicative functions and related constructions, and a big focus on reading and listening as modelling. The aim of this book is to empower the beginner learner with linguistic tools - high-frequency structures and vocabulary - useful for real-life communication. Since, in a typical E.P.I. unit of work, aural and oral work play a huge role, this book should not be viewed as the ultimate E.P.I. coursebook, but rather as a **useful resource** to **complement** your Listening-As-Modelling and Speaking activities.

Sentence Builders – Online Versions

Please note that all these sentence builders will be available in bilingual and Chinese only versions on the Language Gym website, available to download, editable and in landscape design optimised for displaying in the classroom, via the Locker Room section.

How to use this book if you don't know or have NOT bought into our approach

Alternatively, you may use this book to dip in and out of as a source of printable material for your lessons. Whilst our curriculum is driven by communicative functions rather than topics, we have deliberately embedded the target constructions in topics which are popular with teachers and commonly found in published coursebooks.

If you would like to learn about E.P.I. you could read one of the authors' blogs. The definitive guide is Dr Conti's "Patterns First – How I Teach Lexicogrammar" which can be found on his blog (www.gianfrancoconti.com). There are also blogs on Dylan's wordpress site (mrvinalesmfl.wordpress.com) such as "Using sentence builders to reduce (everyone's) workload and create more fluent linguists" which can be read to get teaching ideas and to learn how to structure a course, through all the stages of E.P.I.

Examples of E.P.I. activities and games to play in class, based on MARS EARS sequence, can be found in Simona's padlet (https://en-gb.padlet.com/simograv/svi55fluxeolisi9) "MFL Teaching based on E.P.I. approach, Videos and blogs, Sample activities from Modelling to Spontaneity". These can be used to model tasks.

The book *Breaking the Sound Barrier: Teaching Learners how to Listen* by Gianfranco Conti and Steve Smith, provides a detailed description of the approach and of the listening and speaking activities you can use in synergy with the present book.

The structure of the book

This book contains 10 units which concern themselves with a specific communicative function, such as 'I can say my name and age', 'I can talk about the weather', 'I can say what's in my town'. You can find a note of each communicative function in the Table of Contents. Each unit includes:

- a sentence builder modelling the target constructions, introduced by questions to guide communication;
- a set of Listening-As-Modelling activities to train decoding skills, sound awareness, speech-segmentation, lexical-retrieval and parsing skills;
- a set of reading tasks focusing on both the meaning and structural levels of the text;
- a set of translation tasks aimed at consolidation through retrieval practice;
- a set of writing tasks targeting essential writing micro-skills such as spelling, functional and positional processing, editing and communication of meaning.

Each sentence builder at the beginning of a unit contains one or more constructions which have been selected with real-life communication in mind. Each unit is built around that construction <u>but not solely on it</u>. Based on the principle that each E.P.I instructional sequence must move from modelling to production in a seamless and organic way, each unit expands on the material in each sentence builder by embedding it in texts and graded tasks which contain both familiar and unfamiliar (but comprehensible and learnable) vocabulary and structures. Through lots of careful recycling and thorough and extensive processing of the input, by the end of each unit the student has many opportunities to encounter and process the new vocabulary and patterns with material from the previous units.

Alongside the units you will find: No Snakes No Ladders tasks created to practise speaking skills with an engaging and fun board game that can be photocopied and played in groups of 3 students.

Important *caveat*

1) This is a '**no frills**' book. This means that there are a limited number of illustrations. This is because we want every single little thing in this book to be useful. We have given serious thought to both **recycling** and **interleaving**, in order to allow for key constructions, words and grammar items to be revisited regularly so as to enhance exponentially their retention.

2) **Listening** as modelling is an essential part of E.P.I. The listening files for each listening unit can be found in the AUDIO section on Language-Gym.com - a subscription to the website is **not required** to access these.

3) **All content** in this booklet matches the content on the **Language Gym** website. For best results, we recommend a mixture of communicative, retrieval practice games, combined with Language Gym games and workouts, and then this booklet as the follow-up, either in class or for homework.

4) This booklet is suitable for **beginner** learners. This equates to a **CEFR A1-A2** level, or a beginner **KS2 (or a less strong KS3)** class. You do not need to start at the beginning, although you may want to dip in to certain units for revision/recycling. You do not need to follow the booklet in order, although many of you will, and if you do, you will benefit from the specific recycling/interleaving strategies. Either way, all topics are repeated frequently throughout the book.

We do hope that you and your students will find this book useful and enjoyable.

Table of Contents

UNIT 1 – 我叫

LISTENING

1. Listen and complete with the missing initials

a. wǒ b. nǐ hǎo c. zǎo shang hǎo d. wǒ jiào e. liù f. bā suì

g. jiǔ h. wǒ qī suì i. liǎng suì j. shí yī

2. Break the flow: Draw a line between chunks and add punctuation too (including fullstops)

e.g. 你好!|我叫|Sophia。|我|十岁。

a. 早上好!|我叫|Bobby。|我|八岁。

b. 嗨!|我叫|Charlie。|我|七岁。

c. 你叫|什么名字?|我叫|Janey。

d.你好!|我叫|James。|我|十一岁。

e. 我叫|Anna。|我|九岁。

3. Listen and tick one option for each sentence

a. 2 我叫 An Di b. 1 我两岁 c. 3 我十岁 d. 3 你好，你几岁?

4. Complete with the missing pinyin in the box below

a. nǐ hǎo b. zǎo shang hǎo c. wǒ shíyī suì

d. nǐ jǐ suì e. wǒ jiào Kai f. wǒ jiǔ suì

5. Fill in the grid with the correct name and age

a. 你好，我叫 Mei Ling。我八岁。   **Mei Ling; 8**

b. 早上好，我叫 Joe。我六岁。   **Joe; 6**

c. 你好，我叫 Anna。 我十一岁。   **Anna; 11**

d. 你好吗? 我叫 Kai。我七岁 。   **Kai; 7**

6. Faulty Echo

a. wǒ bā suì. (bu)

b. nǐ hǎo, wǒ wǔ suì. (tǎo as in 讨)

c. zǎo shang hǎo! (sān as in 三)

d. nǐ hǎo, wǒ sì suì. (chī as in 吃)

e. nǐ hǎo, wǒ jiào Sū Fēi (tiào as in 跳)

7. Track the sounds: Listen and write down how many times you will hear the sound

a. jiǔ: **1 time** nǐ hǎo, wǒ jiǔ suì, Anna shí yī suì

b. wǔ: **3 times** wǒ wǔ suì, Li Na wǔ suì, Su Fei shí wǔ suì

c. shí: **5 times** shí yī, bā, jiǔ, shí, shí yī, shí èr, shí

d. hǎo: **4 times** nǐ hǎo, nǐ hǎo ma, zǎo shāng hǎo, wǒ hěn hǎo, nǐ ne

e. jiào: **2 times** nǐ jiào shen me? Wo jiào Wen Jia

8. Spot the Intruder
Highlight the word in each sentence the speaker is NOT saying

e.g. nǐ hǎo, wǒ jiào *Anna*. 你好，我叫安娜。　　　　　　　　wǒ 我

  a. Wǒ jiào Mei. nǐ jiào shén me míng zi? 我叫 Mei。你叫什么名字？　　wǒ 我

  b. nǐ hǎo, wǒ shí èr suì. 你好，我十二岁。　　　　　　　shí 十

  c. zǎo shāng hǎo, wǒ jiào Phillip. 早上好，我叫 Phillip。　　　hǎo 好

  d. nǐ hǎo, nǐ jǐ suì? 你好，你几岁？　　　　　　　　　nǐ 你

Transcript
    e.g 好，叫安娜。

a.　你叫什么名字？叫Mei。

b.　你好，我二岁。

c.　早上，我叫 Phillip。

d.　好，你几岁？

9. Spelling Pinyin Challenge (1-10) Listen and complete the pinyin with the missing initial
a. yī　　b. èr　　c. sān　　d. sì　　e. wǔ　　f. liù　　g. qī　　h. bā　　i. jiǔ　　j. shí

10. Listen and circle the correct number
a. qī; 7　　　　b. shí; 10　　　　c. shí yī; 11　　　　d. wǔ; 5　　　　e. shí ěr; 12

Transcript
e.g 你几岁？我八岁。

a.　你几岁？我七岁。

b.　我十岁。

c.　你几岁？我十一岁。

d.　我五岁。

e.　你几岁？我十二岁。

VOCABULARY BUILDING
1.Match Up
1. e　　2. c　　3. d　　4. b　　5. f　　6. a

2.Missing characters
a. 一　　　　　b. 二　　　　c. 三　　　　　d. 四

3.Complete the sentences with the missing words below
a. 我三岁。　　　　　　b. 我五岁。　　　　　　c. 我四岁。

d. 我十一岁。　　　　　e. 我六岁。　　　　　　f. 我九岁。

4.Sentence Building Blocks
a. 我五岁。　　　　　　　　b. 我两岁。

c. 我叫 Mei, 我八岁。　　　　d. 我叫 An Di, 我十一岁。

READING
1.Honeycomb characters
a . 我叫 Peter。   b. 我十二岁。   c. 我十一岁。

2.True or False
1a. True	1b. True	1c. False (12)	1d. True
2a. False (Stefan)	2b. True	2c. False (11)	2d. False (9)

WRITING
1.Character Jumble
a. 我八岁。   b. 我叫 Maria。   c.我十二岁。   d. 我七岁。   e. 我十一岁。

2.Faulty Translation
a. 我六岁。   b. 你叫什么?   c. 你好吗?   d. 你好!   e. 下午好!

3.Tangled Translation
a. 我叫。。。   b. 你叫什么名字?   c. 我十二岁。   d. 你几岁?

UNIT 2 – PINYIN AND TONES

LISTENING

1. Listen and write the pinyin as you hear it.
No fixed answer. Students write down letters of the alphabet and compare them with their classmates.
Whole-class discussion.

2. Listen and tick the pinyin you hear
Transcript:

1. c	2. m	3. j	4. n	5. a	6. k	7. sh
8. u	9. g					

3. Fill in the gaps: Which sound is it?

a. nǐ   b. wǒ   c. hǎo   d. jiào   e. suì   f. wǔ   g. qī   h. bā

4. Listen and choose the correct pinyin and tones

a. wǔ   b. nǐ   c. jiào   d. shénme   e. jǐ   f. qī   g. liù   h. shí

i. chī   j. sì

5. Put the tone on the correct letter

1. a. bā	b. qī	c. sān	d. yī
2. a. shí	b. shé	c. yú	d. rén
3. a. wǔ	b. nǐ	c. hǎo	d. jiǔ
4. a. liù	b. suì	c. èr	d. jiào

UNIT 3 – 你好吗？

LISTENING

1. Listen and tick the word you hear

e.g. 1 晚上好

a. 1 还好　　　　b. 1 很累　　　　c. 2 很高兴　　　　d. 3 心情不好

2. Listen and complete with the missing letter

a. chī bǎo le　　　　b. jǐn zhāng　　　　c. fēi cháng　　　　d. hěn hǎo

e. wǎn shang hǎo　　　f. xià wǔ hǎo　　　g. xiè xie　　　h. nǐ hǎo, wǒ jiào Robert

i. wǒ bù hǎo　　　j. zǎo shang hǎo　　　k. hěn gāo xìng　　　l. hěn lèi

m. xīn qíng hǎo　　　n. hěn máng

3. Break the flow: Draw a line between words and fill in the punctuation too (including fullstops): Draw a line between words and fill in the punctuation too (including fullstops)

a. 早上好！｜我｜非常好。　　　　　　　b. 下午好！｜我很好，｜因为｜我吃饱了。

c. 晚上好！｜我｜不好，｜因为｜我｜不高兴。　　d. 我还好，｜因为｜我很累。

e. 早上好！我很好，｜因为｜我｜心情好。　　　f. 下午好！｜我很好，｜但是｜我｜很忙。

4. Complete with the missing pinyin

a. hǎo　　　b. wǎn　　　c. hěn　　　d. ān　　　e. bù

f. ma　　　g. lèi　　　h. gāo　　　i. máng　　　j. wèi

5. Listen and choose the correct word or phrase

1. a 早上好　　2. b 下午好　　3. a 晚安　　4. a 紧张　　5. b 不好　　6. b 高兴

6. Fill in the grid with the correct information in English

e.g. An Di; Hello; Happy

a. An Qi; Good morning; extremely well　　　b. Daniel; Good afternoon; Nervous

c. John; Hello; tired　　　　　　　　　　　d. Wei; Good evening; good mood

Transcript

e.g. 你好，我叫 An Di，我很高兴。

a.早上好，我叫 An Qi，我非常好。　　　b.下午好，我叫 Daniel，我很紧张。

c.你好，我叫 John，我很累。　　　　　d.晚上好，我叫 Wei，我心情好。

7. Spot the Intruder. Identify the word in each sentence the speaker is NOT saying

a. 早上好! 我非常好，因为我很高兴。　　　上好

b. 下午好! 我很不好，因为我很累。　　　很

c. 早上好! 我很好，因为我不忙。　　　不

d. 我还好，因为我心情不好。　　　我

e. 你好! 我很不好，因为我很不高兴。　　　你好

f. 我很累，晚安!　　　晚

Transcript

e.g 你好！我很，谢谢！

a. 早！我非常好，因为我很高兴。

b. 下午好！我不好，因为我很累。

c. 早上好！我很好，因为我忙。

d. 还好，因为心情不好。

e. 我很不好，因为我很不高兴。

f. 我很累，安！

8. Tangled Listening- Write the English meaning in the gap
a. Happy   b. How are you?; but   c. Good afternoon; nervous   d. Very well; am in a good mood

VOCABULARY BUILDING

1. Match Up
1. e   2. c   3. f   4. g   5. h   6.a   7.d   8.b

2. Missing Characters
a. 上   b. 下   c. 好

3. Complete with the missing characters
a. 高兴   b. 不   c. 很   d. 很

READING

1. Honeycomb characters
a. 早上好！我很好。   b. 你好！我很不高兴。

2. Read the sentences and complete the grid below in English
a. Amira; 11; well; full   b. Mateo; 13; well; in a good mood
c. Chari; not given; so-so; but tired   d. Si Na; 9; well; but busy   e. Ruyi; 12; not good; nervous

WRITING

1. Character Jumble
a. 我很好。   b. 我叫 Simon。   c. 我很不高兴。

2. Faulty Translation. Spot the difference and correct the Chinese characters
a. 我很**好**。   b. 我很**高兴**。   c. 你叫**什么**？   d. 我**很**好

3. Tangled Translation. Can you fully translate the sentences into Chinese?
a. 我很**好**。   b. 我**不高兴**。   c. 我很**高兴**。   d. 我**很**忙。

e. 我**很**紧张。   f. 我心情**好**。

UNIT 4 – 我的生日

LISTENING

1. Listen and tick the word you hear

1. c   2. b   3. a   4. b   5. c

2. Faulty Echo. You will listen to the sentence twice. The first one is correct, and the second one has an incorrect sound. Underline the wrong sound in each sentence.

e.g. 我六岁 (like lǔ)

a. 我的生日是… (like English Lee)   b. …四月十九日 (like English 'c')

c. 我叫 Kai Nuo (like wō)   d. 六月二十六日 (like English sher)

e. …十月十八日 (like sī)   f. 我二十五岁 (like yī)

3. Break the flow: Draw a line between chunks and fill in the punctuation too (including fullstops)

a. 我的 | 生日 | 是 | 十一月 | 十七日。   b. 我叫 | Ma Li。| 我 | 十二岁。

c. 我的 | 生日 | 是 | 八月 | 四日。   d. 你的 | 生日 | 几月 | 几日？

e. 我的 | 生日 | 是 | 五月 | 二十二日。

4. Fill in the grid with the correct date of birth

a. 15th Jan   b. 18th Sept   c. 24th Oct   d. 27th Nov   e. 5th June

Transcript

e.g. 我的生日是四月十二日。   12th April

a. 我的生日是一月十五日。   15th Jan

b. 你的生日是九月十八日。   18th Sept

c. Chris 的生日是十月二十四日。   24th Oct

d. Kai 的生日是十一月二十七日。   27th Nov

e. Laura 的生日是六月五日。   5th June

5. Spot the Intruder. Identify the word in each sentence the speaker is NOT saying

e.g 我的生日是十二月二日。   生日

a. 我的生日是九月十九日。   日

b. 我十三岁, 我的生日是九月十九日。   岁

c. 你的生日几月几日？   几月

d. 她叫 Li Yun, 她的生日是二月二日。   叫

e. 我的生日是六月十五日。   五

f. 他的生日是十一月三十一日   是

Transcript

e.g 我的是十二月二日。

a. 我的生是九月十九。

THE LANGUAGE GYM

b. 我十三，我的生日是九月十九日。

c. 你的生日几日？

d. 她 Li Yun, 她的生日是二月二日。

e. 我的生日是六月十日

f. 他的生日十一月三十一日

6. Catch it, Swap it: rewrite the wrong word

a. 我**十三**岁…　　　b. 我**三岁**…　　　c. 我的生**日**是…　　　d. ... **你**的生日几月几日？

e. ... 我的生日是**四**月十六日　　　f. ...我的生日是**八**月六日

7. Listen, Tick or Cross

a. X (12 years old)　　b. ✓　　c. X (13 years old, 7th June)　　d. ✓　　e. ✓　　f. X (15th June)

Transcript

e.g. ✓ David 的生日是十二月九日

a. X Peiru 十二岁

b. ✓ Ma sha 的生日是六月七日

c. X Pilar 十三岁，她的生日是七月八日

d. ✓ An Dong 的生日是十一月十七日

e. ✓ Dylan 的生日是十月十八日

f. X Felix 的生日是六月十九日

READING

1. Honecomb characters

a. 三月十四日。　　　b. 六月十六日。　　　　　c. 十二月二十五日。

2. True or False

1.

a. True　　　b. False (good; happy)　　　c. False (7)　　　d. False (19th of September)

2.

a. True　　　b. False (because he is tired)　　c. True　　　d. False (21st of April)

3 Tick or Cross

A.

a. ✓　　　b. X　　　c. ✓　　　d. X　　　e. ✓　　　f. ✓

g. X　　　h. ✓　　　i. ✓　　　j. X　　　k. X

B. Highlight the Chinese in the text above

a. 我叫…　　　b. 我七岁…　　　c. 我的生日是　　　d. …因为我

4. Language Detective

A. Find someone who…

a. Pei Ru　　b. Fen　　c. Pei Ru and Carl　　d. Carl　　e. Veronica　　f. Carl　　g. Pei Ru

B. Odd one out: I am 11 years old. (odd chunk)

WRITING

1. Character Jumble

a. 我的生日是   b. 八月十四日   c. 十二月十一日   d. 十月三十一日

2. Gapped Translation

a. 我**七**岁。   b. 她的生**日**是…   c. 我**不**累。   d. 我很高**兴**。   e. 二**月**十六日   f. **下**午好

3. Split Sentences

a. 3   b. 6   c. 2   d. 1   e. 4   f. 5

4. Rock Climbing

a. 我叫 Feng。我的生日是五月三日。   b. 我十二岁。我的生日是六月三日。

c. 我的生日是三月二十八日。   d. 我十一岁。我的生日是七月十五日。

e. 你的生日几月几日？我的生日是一月一日。

5. Mosaic Translation

a. 我十三岁。我的生日是四月十八日。   b. 你几岁？我十二岁。

c. 我叫 Ana。我的生日是八月二十二日。   d. 你的生日几月几日？我的生日是十二月十六日。

e. 我的生日是十月三十一日。我十一岁。

6. Sentence Puzzle

a. 我的生日是九月十三日。   b. 你的生日是几月几日？   c. 我的生日是二月八日。

d. 他叫 Zen，他九岁。   e. 她的生日是五月十六日。   f. 我叫 Ma Li，我的生日是一月十九日。

7. Tangled Translation

a. Hello, **my name is** Fei. **I am** very well **because I am** happy. **I am** ten **years old. My birthday** is **on the 20th** of January. When is **your birthday?**

b. 你好，**我叫**几米。**我**不好**因为**我很**不高兴**。**我**十一**岁**。**我的生**日是七月**八日**。你的**生日**几月几日？

8. Fill in the Gapss

a. 你好，我**叫** Alexandra。 我非常**好，**因为我**很**高兴。我十四**岁**。我的生日是十**月**八日。

b. 你好，我**叫** Ruben。**我九岁**。我**还**好，**因为**我很累。我的生日是二月二十二日。

c. 下午好，我**叫** Cody。我**十五**岁。我**很**好，因为我心情**好**。我的生日是二月二十**七**日。

9. Pyramid Translation

你好

你好，我叫 Huan。

你好，我叫 Huan。我十岁。

你好，我叫 Huan。我十岁。我的生日是

你好，我叫 Huan。我十岁。我的生日是十月四日。

UNIT 5 – 我的宠物

LISTENING
1. Listen and complete with the missing pinyin
a. yī zhī **m**āo b. yī zhī **g**ǒu c. yī zhī **n**ǐao

d. yī zhī **c**āng shǔ e. yī tiáo **y**ù f. yī tiáo sh**é**

2. Listen and tick the word you hear
a. 1, 3 b. 1, 4 c. 1, 2 d. 1, 2 e. 1, 4
Transcript
a.我有一条鸟 b.我没有蛇 c.我喜欢一只鸟

d.你没有鱼 e.你有宠物吗？

3. Complete with the missing 'a'
a. yì zhī xiǎo māo b. yì zhī hóng sè de niǎo c. yì zhī hēi sè de dà gǒu

d. yì zhī lán sè de tù zi e. yì tíao huáng sè de shé f. yì zhī huī sè de māo

4. Write the missing pinyin as you hear it
a. yì tiáo yú b. yì zhī huī sè de gǒu c. yì zhī hēi sè de tù zi

d. yì zhī bái sè de niǎo e. yì tíao hóng sè de shé f. yì zhī zōng sè de cāng shǔ

5. Faulty echo
a. 我没有狗。（gǔ 古） b. 你有一只蓝色的小鸟。（jiāo 脚）

c. 我没有绿色的鱼。（yǔ 雨） d. 我有一只白色的兔子。（dùzi 肚子）

e. 我没有两只猫（miáo 苗） f. 你有一只小仓鼠。（like English YO）

g. 她喜欢蛇。（like English she） h. 他不喜欢仓鼠。（shù 树）

6. Fill in the grid with the correct information in English
a. Black; Cat b. Grey; Small Snake; c. Brown; Hamster d. Yellow; Small bird
e. Green; Fish f. White; Rabbit g. Brown; Big dog h. Red; Small fish
Transcript
a. 我有一只黑色的猫。 b. 我有一条灰色的小蛇。 c. 我有一只棕色的仓鼠。

d. 我有一只黄色的小鸟。 e. 我有一条绿色的鱼。 f. 我有一只白色的兔子。

g. 我喜欢棕色的大狗。 h. 我喜欢红色的小鱼。

7. Spot the intruder
Identify the word in each sentence the speaker is NOT saying
a.我有一条蓝色的小鱼。 条

b.你有宠物吗？我有一只黑色的大狗。 大

c.我有一只白色的小兔子和一条绿色的蛇。 只

d.我没有红色的小鸟，但是我有一条黄色的鱼。　　　　黄

e.我有一只棕色的小狗，它叫 Skye。　　　　　　　　它

f.他喜欢狗，不喜欢黑色的猫。　　　　　　　　　　　不

g.我不喜欢灰色的大兔子。　　　　　　　　　　　　　的

Transcript

a. 我有一蓝色的小鱼

b. 你有宠物吗？我有一只黑色的狗。

c. 我有一白色的小兔子和一条绿色的蛇。

d. 我没有红色的小鸟，但是我有一条色的鱼。

e. 我有一只棕色的小狗，叫 Skye

f. 他喜欢狗，喜欢黑色的猫。

g. 我不喜欢灰色大兔子。

8. Sentence Bingo. Fill the grid with 4 numbers 1 to 10. You will hear sentences in Chinese. Put a cross in the correct Chinese version to win bingo.

Learners can listen to the recording to hear the 10 sentences read out randomly in Chinese, or read the 10 sentences in English/Chinese themselves, in any order they wish

Transcript (Read in random order)

a.我有一条黄色的小鱼。

b. 我有一条绿色的小蛇。

c. 我有一只黑色的大猫。

e. 我没有白色的仓鼠。

f. 我没有蓝色的鱼。

g. 我有一只棕色的小兔子，它叫 Coco。

h. 我有一只小鸟和一只棕色的狗。

i. 我没有红色的鱼，但是我有黄色的小猫。

j. 我有猫和狗，但是没有兔子。

9. Listening Slalom

e.g. 我有一只黑色的猫　　　　　　(I have a black cat.)

a. 你有红色的鸟　　　　　　　　　(You have a red bird)

b. 我没有黄色的兔子　　　　　　　(I don't have a yellow rabbit.)

c. 他有灰色的狗　　　　　　　　　(He has a grey dog.)

d. 你没有棕色的仓鼠　　　　　　　(You do not have a brown hamster.)

e. 她喜欢蓝色的蛇　　　　　　　　(She likes blue snake)

f. 我没有白色的鱼　　　　　　　　(I don't have a white fish.)

READING

1. Honeycomb character

a. 我有一只大狗。　　　　b. 你有三只小鸟。　　　　c. 我有四条大鱼。

2. Read, Match, Find and Colour
A. Match these sentences to the pictures above
a. Rabbit   b. Snake   c. Hamster   d. Bird   e. Fish   f. Dog
g. Cat   h. Snake   i. Dog   j. Cat

B. Using the sentences in task A find the Chinese for:
a. 黄色的鸟   b. 我有一条红色的小鱼   c. 白色的兔子   d. 喜欢綠色的蛇
e. 灰色的貓   f. 一只小猫   g. 一只大狗   h. 我有一只仓鼠
i. 你没有   j. 我不喜欢

3. True or False
1 a. True   b. False (15th of June)   c. False (a blue fish)   d. True
2 a. False (8)   b. False (13th of May)   c. True   d. False (Mate)
e. False (likes snake)

4. Tick or Cross
A. Read the text. Tick the box if you find the words in the text, cross it if you do not find them
a. ✓   b. X   c. X   d. X   e. X   f. ✓   g. ✓   h. ✓   i. X   j. ✓   k. X
B. Find the Chinese in the text above
a. 我叫…   b. 我的生日是…   c. 小猫   d. 你有宠物吗?   e. 我喜欢它

5. Language Detective
A. Find someone who…
a. Zu Xi   b. Zu Xi   c. Carmen   d. Meng   e. Zu Xi
f. Carmen   g. Nieves   h. Nieves
B. Odd one out: I am 8 years old. (odd chunk)

WRITING

1. Unfinished characters
a. 只   b. 鱼   c. 狗   d. 你

2. Character Jumble
a. 我有一只鸟。   b. 你有一条白色的鱼。   c. 你没有一只大狗。
d. 我有一只小猫。   e. 我没有三条鱼。.

3. Gapped Translation
a. 我九岁。   b. 我有两只小猫。   c. 我没有一条鱼。
d. 你有一只棕色的狗。   e. 她有一条白色的蛇。   f. 我没有宠物。

4. Split Sentences
a. 2   b. 1   c. 3   d. 7   e. 4   f. 5   g. 6

5. Rock Climbing

a. 我有一只狗，它叫 Rocky。　　　b. 我不喜欢宠物。　　　c. 我有两只黑色的猫。

d. 你有一条大蛇。　　　e. 他有五条小鱼。

6. Mosaic Translation

a. 我有一只红色和白色的鸟。　　　b. 我没有猫，但是我有一条蛇。

c. 我有白色的狗，它叫 Lulu。　　　d. 我喜欢大狗，但是不喜欢小猫。

e. 我有一条小鱼，它叫 Wanda。

7. Character Puzzle
A.

a.一只红色的鸟。　　　b. 你有宠物吗?　　　c. 他不喜欢鱼。　　　d. 我有三只大狗。

B.

a. 六条小鱼。　　　b. 我没有蛇。　　　c. 我有两只鸟。　　　d. 她喜欢大狗。

8. Tangled Translation

a. Hello, **my name is** Dylan. I am **seven years old. My birthday** is on the **18th of** July. **I have a** white **big** dog, **it is called** Lily.

b. **你好,** 我叫 Gianfranco。**我九岁。 我的生日是**六月二十日。**我有一条红色的**小鱼。它叫 Nemo。

9. Fill in the Gaps。

a. 你好，我**叫** Si Ning， 我十岁。我的生日是一月六日。我**有**一只狗，**它**叫 Zara。

b. 你好，我叫 Kai Lin，我**十一岁**。我的生日是一月十九日。我有一**条**红色的**小鱼，它**叫 Dory。

c. 早上好，我叫 Mei Ping,， 我十六**岁**。我的**生**日是七月十八**日**。我有两条**白**色的蛇，但**是**没有狗。我喜欢宠物。

10. Guided Translation

a. 我**叫** Robyn, 我十一岁。　　　b. 我**有**一只灰色的兔**子**，**它**叫 Pei Pei 　　。

c. 我**没**有一**只**鸟，但是我有一**只小**仓鼠。　　　d. **你**有一**只**棕**色**的狗和黑色的**猫**。

11. Pyramid Translation

我有

我有一只白色的鸟，

我有一只白色的鸟， 它叫 Dory

我有一只白色的鸟， 它叫 Dory,但是我没有

我有一只白色的鸟， 它叫 Dory,但是我没有黑色的猫。

12. Staircase Translation

a. 你有狗吗?　　　b. 我有白色的鸟。　　　c. 他有一只大猫，它叫 Zar.

d. 我有一只小猫和一只大狗。　　　e. 我有一条小鱼和三只小白狗。

UNIT 6 – 我的书包

LISTENING

1. Faulty Echo
e.g. 我的**书**包里有 (chū instead of shū)

a. 我的**铅**笔盒里有 (jiàn instead of qiān)　　　　　b. 一**支**蓝色的笔 (chī instead of zhī)

c. 一把**白色**的尺子 (pāi sē instead of bāi sè)　　　　d. 一本红色的书 (bèn instead of běn)

e. 一个灰色的**橡皮** (xiān bǐ instead of xiàng pí)

2. Listen and Match
a. 2　　　　　b. 4　　　　　c. 6　　　　　d. 3　　　　　e. 1　　　　　f. 5
Transcript

a.一支笔　　　　b.一把尺子　　　　c.我的书包　　　　d.一个橡皮　　　e.一本书　　　　f.计算器

3. Listen and tick the word you hear
e.g. 我的书包里有**一个橡皮**

a. 3 (我很好)　　b. 1 (一个书包)　c. 2 (一本书)　　d. 1 (一把尺子)
Transcript

a 我很好，你呢?　　　　　b. 我有一个书包。　　　　c.我的书包里有一本书。

d.我的铅笔盒里有一把尺子。

4. Fill in the grid with the correct information in English
e.g. 你好，我叫 Joe，我的书包里有一个红色的计算器。

a. 早上好，我叫 Kai Ren，我的铅笔盒里有一支黑色的笔。

b. 你好，我叫 Kai Di，我的铅笔盒里有一把白色的尺子。

c. 下午好，我叫 An Li，我的书包里有一支粉红色的彩笔。

d. 你好，我叫 Hazel，　我有一支绿色的笔。

Answers

e.g. Red / Calculator

a. **Black / Pen**

b. **Ruler / White**

c. **Pink / Coloured pencil**

d. **Green / Pen**

5. Listen and complete with the missing initials
a. yí gè hēi sè de jì suàn qì　　　　b. yì zhī hóng sè de bǐ　　　　c. yì bǎ lán sè de chǐ zi

d. yì zhī huáng sè de cǎi bǐ

6. Complete with the missing pinyin in the box below
a. lán sè de xiàng pí　　　b. huáng **sè** de **bǐ**　　　c. lù sè de **chǐ** zi　　　d. lán sè de shū

e. qiān **bǐ**　　　　　f. **shū** bāo　　　　g. cǎi **bǐ**　　　　h. wǒ yǒu

7. Break the flow: Draw a line between chunks and add punctuation too (including
a. 我的|铅笔盒里|有|一支|蓝色的|笔。

b. 我的|铅笔盒里|有|一把|黄色的|尺子。

c. 我的|书包里|有|一个|粉红色的|橡皮。

d. 我的|书包里|有|一本|绿色的|书。

e. 我的|铅笔盒里|没有|棕色的|彩笔。

f. 我的|书包里|有|一个|白色的|计算器。

8. Spot the Intruder. Identify the word in each sentence the speaker is NOT saying

a. 我的铅笔盒**里**没有粉红色的铅笔。   里

b. 我的书包里有**一本**绿色的本子。   本

c. 我的书包里有**一把**红色的剪刀。   一把

d. 我的铅笔**盒**里有一本灰色的书。   盒

Transcript

a. 我的铅笔盒没有粉红色的铅笔。

b. 我的书包里有绿色的本子。

c. 我的书包里有红色的剪刀。

d. 我的铅笔里有一本灰色的书。

9. Sentence Bingo

Write any 4 of the letters a to i into the grid below. You will hear sentences in Chinese in a RANDOM ORDER. Tick all 4 of your sentences to win bingo.

Transcript (Read in random order)

a. In my pencil case there is a green pen.   我的铅笔盒里有一支绿色的笔。

b. In my school bag I have a red book.   我的书包里有一本红色的书。

c. In my schoolbag there is a pink calculator.   我的书包里有一个粉红色的计算器。

d. In my pencil case there is a grey exercise book.   我的铅笔盒里有一本灰色的本子。

e. In my school bag I do not have a brown ruler.   我的书包里没有棕色的尺子。

f. In my pencil case there is a blue coloured pencil.   我的铅笔盒里有一支蓝色的彩笔。

g. In my school bag there is a white rubber.   我的书包里有一个白色的橡皮。

h. In my pencil case there is a pencil.   我的铅笔盒里有一支铅笔。

i. In my school bag there is a brown pencil case.   我的书包里有一个棕色的铅笔盒。

10. Listening Slalom

Listen and pick the equivalent English words from each column

a. 我的铅笔盒里有一把黄色的尺子和彩笔。 (In my pencil case there is yellow ruler and coloured pencils.)

b. 我的书包里有一本蓝色的书和本子。 (In my schoolbag there is a blue book and exercise book.)

c. 我的书包里有三只黑色的笔。 (In my schoolbag there are three black pens.)

d. 我的书包里没有白色的橡皮，但是有一支笔。 (In my schoolbag, I don't have a white rubber, but I have a pen.)

e. 我的铅笔盒里没有一把尺子和黑色的橡皮。 (In my pencil case there isn't a ruler and black rubber.)

f. 我的书包里有一本书和一把剪刀。 (In my schoolbag there is a book, and a pair of scissors.)

READING

1. Honeycomb characters

a. 我有一支笔   b. 我有三本书。   c. 我没有尺子。

2. Read, Match, Find and Colour
A. Match these sentences to the pictures above
a. Coloured pencil; Pencil case   b. Schoolbag; book   c. Pencil case; Rubber

d. Pencil case; Pen   e. Schoolbag; Calculator   f. Schoolbag; Ruler   g. Pencil case; Rubber

B. Using the sentences in task A find the Chinese for:
a. 一把蓝色的尺子   b. 我的粉红色的书包   c. 我的铅笔盒里   d. 一个黄色的橡皮

e. 红色的书   f. 有   g. 红色的彩笔   h. 黑色的计算器

i. 没有   j. 我的书包里

3. True or False
A. Read the paragraphs and for each statement answer True of False
a. True   b. False (21st of July)   c. False (dog and cat)   d. True   e. False (red exercise book)   f. True   g. False (9)   h. False (has a rabbit)   i. False (grey pencil)   c. True

B. Find in the text above the Chinese for:
a. 我的生日   b. 一个红色的本子   c. 我的书包里

d. 我没有尺子   e. 我有一只兔子   f. 白色的橡皮

4. Tick or Cross
A. Read the text. Tick the box if you find the words in the text, cross it if you do not find them
a. ✓   b. X   c. X   d. ✓   e. ✓   f. ✓   g. X   h. ✓   i. ✓   j. X   k. ✓   l

B. Find the Chinese in the text above
a. 二月十五日   b. 一本黄色的本子   c. 但是没有橡皮

d. 我的书包里   e. 两把绿色的尺子   f. 我有一只兔子

5. Language Detective
A. Find someone who…
a. 小月   b. Richard   c. 小月   d. 大仁   e. Richard   f. 大仁   g. 大仁

B. Odd one out: A green notebook

WRITING
1. Character Jumble
a. 我有一本白色的书。   b. 你有一只黑色的笔。   c. 你有一本红色的书。

d. 我有一个本子。   e. 我没有笔。

2. Gapped Translation
a. 我有一**支**黄色的铅笔和一把灰色的**尺子**。   b. 我的铅**笔**盒里有一支绿色的彩**笔**和计算器。

c. 我没有**书**包，但是我**有**铅笔盒。   d. **他**的书包里有一本**书**。

3. Split Sentences
a. 2   b. 3   c. 1   d. 5   e. 6   f. 4   g. 7

4. Mosaic Translation
a. 我有一支绿色的笔和一本书。   **b.** 我有一支蓝色的笔和一个白色的橡皮。

c. 我的铅笔盒里有一支黄色的彩笔和一把尺子。   **d.** 我的书包里有一支棕色的彩笔和一个橡皮。

e. 我没有黑色的计算器。　　　　　　　　　　**f.** 我的书包里没有书，但是我有笔。

g. 你没有铅笔盒，但是你有剪刀。

5. Character Puzzle

a. 我的书包里有…　　　　b. 我有两把尺子。　　　　c. 红色的本子。　　　　d. 没有灰色的彩笔。

6. Tangled Translation

a. Hello, **my name is** Josie. **I am** nine years old. My birthday **is the 17th** of January. I have a brown **dog. It is called** Ace. In my pencil case there is **a white rubber and** a red ruler but **there is not** a grey **coloured pencil.**

b. 你好! **我叫** Esther。我十三岁。我的生日是**二月十五日**。我有一只黑色的**猫**叫 Bingo。我的书包里有**一支红色的笔**，但是没有**蓝色的笔**。

7. Fill in the gaps

a. 你好! **我叫** John。**我**十一岁。我的生日是六月二十日。我的**书包**里有一支铅**笔**，一本书和**白色**的橡皮。

b. 你好! **我叫** Carmen。我有**一个**灰色的计算器。我的铅笔盒里**有**一支彩**笔**和**红色**的剪刀，但是你我没有**本子**。

8. Guided Translation

a. 我**的书包**里**有**一支黄**色**的本子。　　　b. 我**的铅笔**盒里**有一支蓝色**的**铅笔**。

c. 我**的铅笔**盒里**没**有橡皮。　　　d. 我**没有**尺子，**但**是我有一本**书**。

9. Pyramid Translation

My

My school bag inside

My school bag inside there is a green book

My school bag inside there is a green book and a red exercise book,

My school bag inside there is a green book and a red exercise book, but I don't have a ruler.

10. Staircase Translation

a. 我有一支红色的笔。　　　　　b. 你有白色的书包。

c. 我的书包里有一支蓝色的笔和一把尺子。　　　d. 我没有笔，但是我有一本书。

e. 我的书包里没有书，但是我有一一本红色的本子。

UNIT 7 - 你是哪国人？

LISTENING

1. Listen and tick the word you hear
a. 1 (英国人)   b. 3 (我会说)   c. 2 (中文)   d. 3 (澳大利亚人)
Transcript
a.我是**英国人**   **b.我会说**英语   **c.** 我会说一点**中文**   **d.**我是英国人，也是**澳大利亚人**

2. Fill in the grid with the correct information in English
a. Ronan; France (French); French   b. Albert; Australia (Australian); Arabic (doesn't speak)
c. Pamela; UK (British); Spanish   d. Kai Lin; France (French); German (a little)
e. Li Chun; UK (British); Japanese (a little)   f. Su Rui; China (Chinese); English
g. Arun; USA (American); Chinese
Transcript
a.   他叫 Ronan, 他是法国人，他会说法语。

b.   他叫 Albert, 他是澳大利亚人，他不会说阿拉伯语。

c.   我叫 Pamela，我是英国人，我会说一点西班牙语。

d.   她叫 Kai Lin, 她是法国人，她会说一点德语。

e.   她叫 Li Chun, 她是英国人，她会说一点日语。

f.   我叫 Su Rui, 我是中国人，我会说英语。

g.   他叫 Arun, 他是美国人，他会中文。

3. Listen and complete with the missing pinyin
a. wǒ **shì** měi guó rén.   b. wǒ **shì** zhōng guó rén.   c. wǒ **huì** shuō yì diǎn fǎ **yǔ**.

d. wǒ **shì** yīng guó rén.   e. nǐ shì nǎ guó rén?   f. wǒ **huì** shuō yīng **yǔ**.

g. wǒ **bú huì** shuō rì yǔ.   h. wǒ yě huì shuō zhōng **wén**.   i.**tā** shì ào dà lì yǎ rén.

j. dàn **shì** wǒ bú **huì** shuō dé yǔ.

4. Split sentences. Listen and match
a. 5   b. 3   c. 7   d. 2   e. 1   f. 4   g. 6
Transcript
a.   我叫 Mag。

b.   我说英语。

c.   我说法语, 也会说中文。

d.   我不是中国人。

e.   你是哪国人？

f.   我是英国人。

g.   也会说一点中文。

5. Break the flow: Draw a line between chunks and add punctuation too (including

a. 我是|美国人，|我说|中文,|也会说|一点|法语。

b. 我是|德国人。|我说|德语。

c. 我是|日本人。|我说|日语，|也会说|德语。

d. 我是|澳大利亚人，|我说|一点|西班牙语。

e. 我说|中文，|也会说|一点|阿拉伯语。

6. Spot the Intruder. Identify the word in each sentence the speaker is NOT saying

a. 我是<u>英</u>国人，我说一点德语　　。　　　　　**英**

b. 我是澳大利亚人，我说一点阿拉伯<u>语</u>。　　**语**

c. 我是法国<u>人</u>，但是不会说法语。　　　　　**人**

d. 我说中文，<u>也</u>会说西班牙语。　　　　　　**也**

e. 我是澳大利亚人，我说<u>一点</u>中文。　　　　**一点**

f. 我是日本人。我<u>说</u>中文，也会说日语。　　**说、说**

g. 我不是中国人，<u>但是</u>我会说中文。　　　　**但是**

h. 我是英国<u>人</u>，我十一岁，我<u>说</u>中文。　　**人、说**

7. Catch it, Swap it

Listen, spot the difference between what you hear and the written text and edit each sentence accordingly.

Transcript:

a. 我是<u>美</u>国人，也会说一点法语。　　　　　**英国**

b. 我是澳大利亚人，<u>我说一点</u>阿拉伯语。　　**也会说一点**

c. 我是<u>中国人</u>，我说一点英语。　　　　　　**法国人**

d. 我是日本人，<u>但是</u>不会说日语。　　　　　**但是**

e. 我说西班牙<u>语</u>，也<u>会说一点</u>德语。　　　**说一点**

f. 我是中国人，<u>我说</u>中文。　　　　　　　　**但是会**

Transcript

a. 我是英国人，也会说一点法语。

b. 我是澳大利亚人，也会说阿拉伯语。

c. 我是法国人，我说一点英语。

d. 我是日本人，不会说日语。

e. 我说西班牙语，也会说德语。

f. 我是中国人，但是会说中文。

8. Sentence Bingo Teachers can listen to the recording to hear the 10 sentences read out randomly in Chinese, or read the 10 sentences in English/Chinese themselves, in any order they wish.

9. Listening Slalom

a. 我叫 Chris, 我是法国人，但是我不会说法语。　(My name is Chris, I am French but I can't speak French.)

b. 你好，我是澳大利亚人，但是我不会说英语。　(Hello I am Australian but I can't speak English.)

c. 她是英国人，她会说中文，也会说阿拉伯语。　(She is British she can speak Chinese she can also speak Arabic)

d. 我会说日语，一点中文。我是德国人。(I can speak Japanese, a little Chinese I am German)

e. 我不会说德语。我会说英语，也会说一点阿拉伯语。(I can't speak German. I can speak English and can also a little Arabic)

f. 我不是日本人，我是西班牙人,但是我会说西班牙语。(I am not Japanese I am Spanish But I can speak Spanish)

READING

1. Honeycomb Characters

a. 我是中国人。我九岁。我会说英语。   b. 我是中国人，但是我不会说中文。

c.他是英国人。他十岁。他会说中文。

2. True or False
A. Read the paragraphs below and answer True or False

a. True   b. False (bird)   c. False (Spanish)   d. True
e. False (he can speak a little Chinese)   f. True   g. False (12 years old)   h. True   i.
True   j. False (she likes speaking in Chinese)

B. Find in the text above the Chinese for:

a. 它两岁   b. 我喜欢   c. 它很好

d. 也会说一点   e. 我没有宠物   f. 早上好

3. Tick or Cross
A. Read the text. Tick the box if you find the words in the text, cross it if you do not find them

a. X   b. X   c. ✓   d. ✓   e. ✓   f. X   g. X   h. X   i. ✓   j. X   k. ✓   l. ✓

B. Find the Chinese in the text above

a. 十月十五日   b. 也会说英语   c. 我很不喜欢说西班牙语

d. 但是不会说法语   e. 我很喜欢说德语

4. Language Detective
A. Find someone who…

a. Ming Wen   b. Ming Wen   c. Richard   d. Richard & Ming Wen
e. Richard   f. Richard & Cindy   g. Cindy

B. Odd one out
I don't like to speak English

WRITING

1. Character Jumble

a. 我说中文。   b. 我是英国人。   c. 我不会说日语。

d. 我也会说法语。   e. 我会说一点中文

2. Gapped Translation

a. 我会说**中文**和**英语**，但是不会说德语。I speak **Chinese** and **English,** but I can't speak **German.**

b. 他是**中国人**，也会说**一点**西班牙语。He is **Chinese** and I can also speak **a little** Spanish.

c. 我是**英国人**，但是**不会**说英语。I am **British** but I **cannot** speak English.

d. 你会说**中文**吗? 我会说**日**语。Can you speak **Chinese**? I speak **Japanese.**

3. Split Sentences

a. 4   b. 2   c. 6   d 3   e. 1   f. 5

4. Rock Climbing

a. 他是法国人，但是不会说法语。   b. 我说中文，但是不会说日语。

c. 你会说中文吗？，我会说英语。   d. 你是哪国人？我是英国人。

e. 我说一点德语，也会说阿拉伯语。

5. Mosaic Translation

a. 我会说日语，但是不会说中文。 I can speak Japanese, but can't speak Chinese

b. 你是哪国人？我不是中国人。 What is your nationality? I am not Chinese.

c. 你会说英语吗？我不会说英语。 Can you speak English? I can't speak English.

d. 我说英语，也会说西班牙语。 I can speak English and can also speak Spanish

e. 她会说一点阿拉伯语，也会说一点日语。 She can speak a little Arabic and can also speak a little Japanese.

6. Fill in the Gapss

a. 你好！我叫 Robert。我**八**岁。我的生日是六**月**二十日。我是**英国人**。我说**一点**德语和阿拉伯语，**也**会说**中文**。

b.你好！我叫子乐。我有一只**大**狗。它**叫** Frankie。我**说**德语和西班牙语，也会说**一点**法语。我**也**喜欢说日语。

7. Tangled Translation

a. Hello, **my name is** Mi Mi. **I am** seven years old. My birthday **is on the 13**[th] of March. **I am French.** I speak French and English. **I also speak a little** Italian, **but** I don't speak **Japanese.** I like **Chinese.**

b.早上好！**我叫** Laura。**我**十一岁。我的生日**是**四月**四日**。我有**一只狗**，**它叫** Treacle。我是**中国人**。**我会说**英文，**也会说一点法文**，但是**我不会说日文**。

8. Sentence Puzzle

a. 我说**英**语和**中文**。   b. **她**也会**说**中文**吗**？。   c.**他**是日**本**人。

9. Guided Translation

a. 嗨！我**叫**小月。我**是**中国人。   b. **他**是英国人，**他**说一点德语。

c. 我**说**法语，也**会**说一点**日**语。   d. 我**说**阿拉伯语，但**是**不会说**法**语。

10. Pyramid Translation

你好！

你好！我叫 Lu Xi。

你好！我叫 Lu Xi。我会说中文，

你好！我叫 Lu Xi。我会说中文，也会说一点英语，

你好！我叫 Lu Xi。我会说中文，也会说一点英语，但是我不会说法语。

11. Staircase Translation

a. 我是中国人。   b. 我说英语和法语。   c. 我不会说英语，但是我会说中文。

d. 我说一点日语，但是我不会说法语。   e. 我是英国人。我说一点中文，但我不会说日语。

UNIT 8 – 天气怎么样？

LISTENING

1. Listen and tick the word you hear

a. 2 (今天香港**是晴天**) b. 1 (昨天西班牙**很热**) c. 3 (有时候英国**下雨**)

d. 1 (昨天中国**天气好**) e. 2 (这个月北京**多云**)

Transcript

a. 今天香港**是晴天**。

b. 昨天西班牙**很热**。

c. 有时候英国**下雨**。

d. 昨天中国**天气好**。

e. 这个月北京**多云**。

2. Faulty echo

e.g. 今天是**晴天** *(晴 like 请)*

a. 昨天**中**国很冷 (中 like 虫) b. 明天台北有**风** (风 like English 'fern')

c. 今天北京多**云** (多云 like 多鱼) d. **这**个月上海下雨 (这 like 'jay')

e. 有时候英国**天气好** (天 like 甜) f. **今天**天气怎么样？(今天 like 晴天)

3. Listen and Match

a. 3 b. 5 c. 2 d. 4 e. 1

Transcript

a. 今天北京很热 b. 这个星期英国下雨 c. 昨天中国下雪 d. 明天西安多云

e. 有时候上海天气好

4. Listen and complete with the missing initial

a. Jīn tiān tiān **q**ì hǎo b. Běijīng **x**ià **y**ǔ c. Jiā ná dà **x**ià **x**uě

d. Tái běi **h**ěn **r**è e. **z**uó tiān **x**iāng gǎng… f. **m**íng tiān shǐ **q**íng tiān

5. Break the flow: Draw a line between words and fill in the punctuation too (including fullstops)

a. 昨天|英国|天气|怎么样？|是晴天。 b. 这个月|台北|非常热。

c. 这个星期|日本|天气好|非常热。 d. 有时候|中国上海|有一点冷。

6. Complete with the missing pinyin in the box below

a. tiān qì hǎo b. jīn tiān hěn rè c. zuó tiān d. yǒu fēng

e. duō yún f. xià xuě

7. Fill in the grid with the correct information in English

e.g. Yesterday; good

a. Sometimes; windy b. Tomorrow; sunny c. This month; rainy

d. This week; cold e. Today; hot

Transcript

e.g. 昨天北京天气好。

a. 有时候中国多风

b. 明天台北是晴天

c. 这个月上海下雨

d. 这个星期澳大利亚很冷

e. 今天香港很热

8 Spot the Intruder. Identify the word in each sentence the speaker is NOT saying

a. 今天中国天气<u>不</u>好。　　　　　　　　　　不

b. 有时候北京<u>下</u>雪。　　　　　　　　　　　下

c. 明天<u>非常</u>冷。　　　　　　　　　　　　非常

d. 这个<u>星期</u>上海下雨。　　　　　　　　　星期

9. Listening Slalom

e.g. 今天北京非常热　　　　　　　*e.g.* Today is extremely hot Beijing

a. 这个月台北天气好　　　　　　　This month it is good weather in Taipei.

b. 昨天西安下雨　　　　　　　　　Yesterday it rained in Xi'an.

c. 明天上海天气不好.　　　　　　Tomorrow it is bad weather in Shanghai.

d. 今天英国很冷　　　　　　　　　Today it is cold in the UK.

e. 有时候香港是晴天　　　　　　　Sometimes it is sunny in Hong Kong.

f. 这个星期中国下雪　　　　　　　This week there is snow in China.

g. 今天印度有风　　　　　　　　　Today it is windy in India.

READING

1. Honeycomb characters

a. 你好，今天中国很冷　　　　　b. 你好，英国天气不好

2. True or False (map)

a. False　b. False　　　c. False　　　d. True

e. False　　　　f. True　　　g. True　　　h. True

3. Read, Match, Find and Colour

A. Match the sentences to the pictures above

a. It snows　　　　b. It's sunny　　　c. It rains　　　d. It rains

e. It's windy　　　f. It's nice weather　　g. It's cloudy　　h. It's hot

i. It's good weather　　j. It's cold

B. Using the sentences in task A to find the Chinese for:

a. 很热　　　b. 多云　　　c. 这个月　　d. 天气好　　e. 这个星期　　f. 非常冷

g. 下雨　　　h. 今天　　　i. 晴天　　　j. 有风

4. True or False

A. Read the paragraphs below and answer True or False

a. False (10)　　　　　　　　　　　b. True

c. False (He is French)　　　　　　d. True

e. False (it is not good)　　　　　　f. True

g. False (She is from the UK)   h. True
i. False (She speaks English and a bit of Chinese)   j. True

B. Find in the texts above the Chinese for:

a. 但是今天...   b. 非常热   c. 今天是晴天   d. 但是今天天气不好

5. Language Detective
A. Read & answer the questions

a. Ruyi   b. Ruyi   c. In Beijing; in Spain   d. In the UK
e. In Beijing   f. Oscar   g. In Spain

B. Two are odd

I am from the UK & I have a white and grey cat

WRITING

1. Unfinished characters

a. 天气**好**   b. 今**天有风**   c. 有一**点**热   d. **昨**天下雨

2. Gapped Translation

a. 我是中国人。这个**月**西安**天气**好。I **am** Chinese. This **month** the weather is good in Xian.

b. 昨**天**台北多**云**。It was **cloudy** in Taipei **yesterday.**

c. 有时候**英国**天气**不好**。**Sometimes**, it is not **good** weather in the UK.

3. Fill in the gaps

a. 你好，我**叫** Ling。我**十四**岁。我**是**中国**人**。西安**天气**好，但是今天**有风**，也非常冷。

b.你好，我**叫** Zhu Li。我的生日是五月三日。我十**岁**。我是上海**人**。这个**月**的天气好，但是今天**多云**，也下雨。

UNIT 9 – 我家

LISTENING

1. Listen and tick the word you hear
a. 1 b. 3 c. 1 d. 2 e. 1 f. 3

Transcript

a. 我住在西安。 b. 我爱香港。 c. 天津很美。

d. 我的城市不小。 e. 我的城市很无聊。 f. 我的城市很丑。

2. Faulty Echo

e.g. 我住在北京。 *(在 like 菜)*

a. 我住在伦敦。(住 like 出) b. 我喜欢我家，因为很大。(大 like dai)

c. 我不喜欢我家，因为很吵。(不 like English boo) d. 我爱我家，因为很安静。(家 like 假)

3. Listen and complete with the missing pinyin

a. wǒ zhù **z**ài shàng hǎi b. wǒ zhù zài **t**ái **b**ěi c. wǒ de **ch**éng shì

d. wǒ **t**ǎo yàn … e. **r**én tài **d**uō le f. yīn wèi **h**ěn rè **n**ào

g. wǒ **a**ì wǒ jiā h. wǒ **b**ù xǐ huan wǒ jiā i. yīn wèi hěn **ch**ǎo

j. yīn wèi hěn an jìng

4. Narrow Listening. Gap-fill

a.你好！我叫大中。我**十一**岁。我是**英国**人，但是我住**在**中国。我会说**一点**法语，也会说**英语**和**中文**。我很喜欢我家，**因为**很安静。

b.早上好！我叫安！我**八**岁。我是西班牙**人**，但是我住在德**国**。我**会**说西班牙**语**和德语。**我的**城市**很**大，但是**很**吵。

5. Fill in the grid with the correct information in English

a. Erin; likes it; beautiful b. An Dong Ni; doesn't like it; small
c. Stephanie; loves it; lively d. Yi Hua; likes it; big
e. Rory; loves it; quiet

Transcript

a.   你好！我叫 Erin。我喜欢我的城市，因为很美。

b.   嗨！我叫 An Dong Ni。我是中国人，我住在香港，但是我不喜欢我的城市，因为很小。

c.   下午好！我叫 Stephanie。我是德国人，我住在台北。我爱我家，因为很热闹。

d.   晚上好！我叫 Yi Hua。我是中国人，我住在上海。我喜欢我的城市，因为很大。

e.   你好！我叫 Rory。我是英国人。我爱我住的小区，因为很安静。

6. Complete with the missing pinyin in the box below

a. **w**ǒ jiā 我家 b. **w**ǒ xǐ huan 我喜欢 c. **w**ǒ de chéng shì 我的城市 d. **w**ǒ bù xǐ huan 我不喜欢

e. **w**ǒ tǎo yàn 我讨厌 f. yīn wèi 因为 g. hěn dà 很大 h. hěn xiǎo 很小

i. hěn měi 很美 j. hěn ān jìng 很安静

7. Spot the Intruder. Identify the word in each sentence the speaker is NOT saying

a. 因为　　　　b. 住　　　　c. 我的　　　　d. 我喜欢　　　　e. 也　　　　f. 不

Transcript:

a. 我住在伦敦。我不喜欢我家，不美。

b. 我在西安。我不喜欢我的城市，因为很吵。

c. 我住在上海。我喜欢城市，因为很热闹。

d. 我的城市，因为很安静。

e. 你家在哪里？我住在北京。我喜欢我的城市，因为很大，很热闹。

f.我喜欢我的城市，因为人太多了。

8. Catch it, Swap it. Listen, spot the difference and edit each sentence accordingly

e.g **美**=安静　　　　a. **城市**=家; **美** = 不美　　b. **美**= 吵　　　　c.**他**=我

Transcript:

e.g 我喜欢我的城市，因为很**安静**。

a. 我不喜欢我的**家**，因为很**不美**。　　　　　　b. 我讨厌我的城市，因为非常**吵**。

c. **我**不喜欢我家，因为很吵。

9. Sentence Bingo. Fill the grid with 4 numbers 1 to 10. The recording will play the Chinese sentences in a random order. Tick all 4 of your sentences to win.

Transcript <u>(read in random order)</u>

1. 我爱我的城市，因为很大。　　　　2. 我不喜欢我的城市。

3. 我喜欢我的城市。　　　　4. 我爱我家，因为很美。

5. 我喜欢我的家，因为很大。　　　　6. 我不爱我的城市，因为很吵。

7. 我不喜欢我家，因为很小。　　　　8. 我不喜欢我的城市，因为不美。

9. 我讨厌我的城市，因为很大。　　　　10. 我爱我的城市，因为很热闹。

10. Listening Slalom

Transcript:

e.g. 我叫 Joshua。 我住在香港，我爱我的城市。My name is Joshua. I live in Hong Kong. I love my city.

a. 我住在天津。我爱我的城市，因为很热闹。I live in Tianjin. I love my city because it is lively.

b. 我住在上海，我喜欢我的城市，因为很美。I live in Shanghai, I like my city because it is beautiful.

c. 我不喜欢我家，因为很小。 I dont like my home because it is small.

d. 我喜欢我家，因为很美，也很安静。I like my home because it is beautiful and also quiet.

e. 我讨厌我的城市，因为不美，也很无聊。I hate my city because it's not beautiful and also boring.

f. 我住在伦敦。我家很大、很吵，也很热闹。I live in London. It is big, nosiy and lively.

READING

1. Honeycomb Characters

a. 我喜欢我的城市。　　　　　　b. 我住在中国。我爱我家因为很大。

2. True or False
A. Read the paragraphs below and answer True or False
Mai Ke
a. False (five)   b. False (English)   c. True   d. False (it is hot)
e. True   f. False (big and lively)
Vani
g. True   h. False (a little cold)   i. False (she lives in London)
j. False (pretty and not boring)
B. Find in the text above the Chinese for:
a. 非常热   b. 这个月   c. 因为很美
d. 很大，也很热闹   e. 我爱我的城市   f. 我住在

3. Tick or Cross
A. Read the text. Tick the box if you find the words in the text, cross it if you do not find them
Paddy   a. ✓   b. X   c. X   d. X   e. ✓   f. ✓
Bai Jia   g. X   h. ✓   i. ✓   j. X   k. X   l. ✓   m. ✓
B. Find the Chinese in the texts above
a. 今天北京下雨。   b. 我喜欢安静的城市。   c. 昨天上海下雪。
d. 我讨厌我的城市，因为很吵。   e. 因为很热闹，但是有一点吵。

4. Language Detective
A. Find someone who…
a. Patrick   b. Rui Qui   c. Rui Qui, Li Cha   d. Patrick   e. Patrick.   f.Li Cha
g. Rui Qui, Li Cha
B. Odd one out: I like my home

WRITING

1. Character Jumble
a. 我住在北京。   b. 我不喜欢我家。   c. 因为很安静。   d. 我爱我的城市
e. 因为人太多了。

2. Gapped Translation
a. 我**是**澳大利亚人，但是我**住**在中国。 I **am** Australian but I **live** in China.
b. 我喜欢我的城市，因**为**很美，**也**很**大**。 I like my city **because** it is very pretty and **also** very **big**.
c. 我住**在**伦敦。我爱**我**的城市。 I live **in** London. I love **my** city.

3. Split Sentences
a. 7   b. 6   c. 4   d. 3   e. 1   f. 5   g. 2

4. Rock Climbing
a. 我是英国人，但是我住在中国。   b. 我不喜欢我的城市，因为很吵。
c. 你喜欢你家吗？不，因为很小。   d. 我喜欢香港，因为非常好。
e. 你住在哪里？我住在台北。

5. Mosaic Translation

a. 我的城市很美，也很小，但是很热闹。

b. 你住在哪里？我住在一个大城市。

c. 我不喜欢我的城市，因为不美。

d. 你喜欢你的城市吗？我爱台北。

e. 我家很安静，也很美。但是也很小。

6. Fill in the Gaps

a. 你好，我叫 Sam。 我十二岁。我是中国人，但是我住在英国。我会说一点德语。我喜欢我家，因为很安静。

b. 你好，我叫 Maai。 我是日本人，但是我住在格拉斯哥。我会说日语和中文，也会说一点英语。我爱我的城市，因为很美，也非常热闹。

7. Tangled Translation

a. Hello, **my name is** Wei Min. **I am** Chinese, **but** I live **in Japan.** I speak German **and Japanese. Today,** the weather **is good,** it is **windy,** also **sunny.** I live **in a big city, but** I don't like it **because it is extremely** big and **noisy.**

b. 早上好，我叫正. 我十一岁， 我没有宠物. 我住在西安。 我喜欢我的城市因为 很大，也很美。 我也爱我的城市因为很热闹。 这个月西安的天气好，不冷不热。

8. Guided Translation

a. 你好,我叫 Patricia。 我住在中国。

b. 我是西班牙人。 我会说英语。

c. 我的城市不大。 我喜欢我的城市因为很安静。

d. 我的城市很热闹， can 不无聊。

e. 你住在哪里?

9. Pyramid Translation

你好,

你好, 我叫 Ya Lun。

你好, 我叫 Ya Lun。我住在台北。

你好, 我叫 Ya Lun。我住在台北。我喜欢我的城市因为很大，

你好, 我叫 Ya Lun。我住在台北。我喜欢我的城市因为很大，也很很美。

10. Staircase Translation

a. 我喜欢我的城市。

b. 我不喜欢我家，因为不美。

c. 我爱我家，因为很小，也很安静。

d. 我讨厌我的城市，因为很大，不美，也很吵。

e. 我非常喜欢我的城市，因为很大，不小，也很安静。

UNIT 10 – 我住的地方
LISTENING

1. Listen and tick the word you hear
a. 2 (广场 square)   b. 1 (电影院 cinema)   c. 2 (没有 don't have)   d. 3 (饭馆 restaurant)

2. Faulty Echo
e.g. 我的城市<u>有</u>游泳池。 (English: you)

a. 我<u>住</u>的地方有一个公园。 (zhū)

b. 我住的<u>小区</u>有太多商店和饭馆。 (English: 'q')

c. 我的城市有<u>饭馆</u>和超市。 (fāng)

d. 我住的地方没<u>有游泳</u>池。 (yǒu yòng)

e. 我的城市有运动<u>中心</u>，也有城堡。 (zǒng jīng)

3. Listen and complete with the missing pinyin (initials)
a. fēi **j**ǐ **ch**ǎng   b. **ch**éng bǎo   c. huǒ **ch**ē **zh**àn   d. **sh**āng diàn

e. **ch**āo **sh**ì   f. **j**iào táng

4. Complete with the missing pinyin in the box below
a. yī gè y**óu** y**ǒn**g chí   b. yě y**ǒu**   c. y**ǒu** hěn d**uō**   d. g**ōn**g yuán

e. h**uǒ** chē zhàn   f. yùn d**òn**g zh**ōn**g xīn

5. Fill in the grid with the information in English
a. church; x beach   b. Shops, bank; x university
c. Schools, hospital; x swimming pools   d. Supermarket, library; x cinema
Transcript
a. 我住的地方有一个教堂，但是没有海滩。
b. 我住的小区有很多商店和银行，但是没有大学。
c. 我住的城市有好几个学校和医院，但是没有游泳池。
d. 我住的小区有一个超市和图书馆，但是没有电影院。

6. Spot the Intruder. Identify the word in each sentence the speaker is NOT saying
a. 很多   b. 我的   c. 也   d. 两个
Transcript
a. 我的城市有饭馆和学校。   b. 我喜欢城市，因为有大学和飞机场。
c.我住的小区有图书馆，有游泳池。   d. 我住的地方有火车站，也要好几个公园。

7. Narrow Listening. Gap-fill
我住在中国的一个**大**城市。我住的地方有三个**电影院**，一个有游泳**池**和饭馆。我喜欢我的**小区**，**因为** 很**安**静，**也**很漂亮。

8. Listening Slalom

a. 我的城市有一个运动中心和博物馆。   In my city there is a sport centre and a museum.

b. 我家在中国，我住的地方有火车站和学校。I live in China, where I live thre is a train station and a school.

c. 我的城市有很多商店，但是没有游泳池。In my city there are many shops, but there are no swimming pools.

d. 我爱我的小区，因为很热闹，有饭馆，也有商店。I love my neighbourhood becasue it is lvely, there are restaurants and shops

e. 我喜欢我的城市，因为很漂亮，有广场，但是没有运动中心。I like my city because it is pretty, there is a square, but there isn't a sport centre.

f. 我住的地方没有超市，也没有图书馆。Where i live there isn't a supermarket, there is also no library.

READING

1. Honeycomb characters

a. 我的城市有两个大学。

b. 我住的小区没有公园。

2. True or False

A. Read the paragraphs below and then answer True or False

a. True

b. False (he likes)

c. False (big and lively)

d. True

e. False (no cinemas)

f. False (she is from France)

g. False (in China)

h. False (it is hot)

i. True

j. False (no post offices)

B. Find in the text above the Chinese for:

a. ...因为很美

b. 有一个火车站

c. 我喜欢我的城市

d. 没有电影院

3. Tick or Cross

A. Read the text. Tick the box if you find the words in the text, cross it if you do not find them

a. ✓   b. X   c. X   d. X   e. X   f. ✓   g. X   h. ✓   i. X   j. ✓   k. ✓   l. X

B. Find the Chinese in the text above

a. 一个小城市

b. 没有飞机场

c. 我住的城市叫西安

d. 我住的小区有公园

e. 但是没有城堡

4. Language Detective

A. Find someone who...

a. Lilian & Roberto

b. Ma Hong

c. Ma Hong

d. Roberto

e. Ma Hong

f. Lilian

g. Roberto

B. Odd one out:

I don't like my city.

WRITING

1. Unfinished characters!

a. 火车**站**

b. 商**店**

c. **超市**

d. **饭**馆

e. **图书馆**

f. **运动**中心

g. 有一个**公园**

2. Gapped Translation

a. 我住的**小区**有运动中心和**公园**。In my **neighbourhood** there is a sports centre and a **park**.

b. 我的城市有**两个**大**广场**。In my city there are **two** big **squares.**

c. 我**住在**伦敦。伦敦有**好几个**教堂和城堡。I **live** in London. In London there are **several** churches **and** castles.

d. 你住的小区有**什么**？有一个很美的**火车**站。**What is** there in your neighbourhood? There is a beautiful **train** station.

e. 我**住的**地方有**一个**博物馆**和**学校。**Where** I live there is **a** museum **and** schools.

3. Split Sentences

a. 4   b. 1   c. 2   d. 3   e. 5   f. 6

4. Rock Climbing

a. 我住的小区有图书馆和城堡。

b. 我的城市有医院和飞机场。

c. 我住的地方没有银行，也没有学校。

d. 你住的城市有什么？有一个大广场和一个公园。

e. 我不喜欢我住的小区，因为没有电影院。

5. Fill in the gaps

a. 你好，我叫 Ram。我九岁。我是西班牙**人**，但是我**住在**伦敦。我喜欢住我住的地方，因为非常大，有游泳**池**，**也有**运动**中心**。

b. 你好，我**叫** Nieves。我是美**国**人，但是我住在中国北京。我喜欢我的城**市**，**因为**天气好。我的城市有**好几**个教堂，也有大学。

6. Tangled Translation

a. Hello, **my name is** Ana. **I live in** the UK, but **I** am **Chinese.** I speak English **and Chinese.** In the UK, the **weather** is **often not** good. **In my neighbourhood** there is **a school** and shops, **but** there is no **train station.**

b. 你好，**我叫** Juan。我十二岁。我住在**中国**。我住的的**城市叫**北京。**我喜欢**我的城市，因为**很大**，也很热闹。**我的**小区**有**电影院**和商店**，但是没有公园。

7. Guided Translation

a. 嗨！我**叫** Yong Kang。我**住在一个**很**美**的城**市**叫台北。

b. 我住**在**一个**大**城市。我**的**城市有商**店**，**但是没**有**海**滩。

c. 我**住**的小**区**有**学**校和教**堂**，但是没有公**园**，很**无聊**。

8. Change one thing. Make a New sentence by changing one word/phrase

No fixed answer. Students write down their sentences and compare them with their classmates. Whole-class discussion.

9. Staircase Translation

a. 我喜欢我的城市。

b. 我不喜欢我住的地方，因为没没有大学。

c. 我住的小区很美，有图书馆，但是没有运动中心。

d. 我的城市很大，也很吵。有很多商店，但是没有公园。

e. 我的家乡小，也很安静，但是很美。有学校，但是没有大学。